D0876560

Pasquala

The Story of a
California Indian Girl

11-5-94

To Renee — With
fondest memories
of fifth grade at
Rancho Romero!

Michele Lasagna
(of course, I'll always
remember you!)
Love, Gail Faber

quala

The Story of a
California Indian Girl

by
Gail Faber and Michele Lasagna
Magpie Publications/Alamo, California

Acknowledgements

The authors would like to thank the following persons for their generous contribution of time and effort in editing this book:

Andrew Andreoli, Consultant for American Indian Education, California State Department of Education.

Carol Green, Children's Author.

John Johnson, Curator of Anthropology, Santa Barbara Museum of Natural History.

Monna Latta Olson, Writer, Editor, Publisher.

Sharon Marocchi, Teacher, San Ramon Valley Unified School District, Danville, California.

Special thanks for art and word processing assistance to Lou Ann Styles, Judith McCarty, and Florence Cahill.

Copyright © 1990 by Gail Faber and Michele Lasagna. All rights reserved. No part of this work, including text, illustrations, maps, etc. may be reproduced or transmitted in any form.

All illustrations are property of Gail Faber and Magpie Publications, Copyright © 1990.

First Edition August 1990

Published by Magpie Publications
Box 636
Alamo, CA 94507

ISBN: 0-936480-06-8 Student soft cover edition
ISBN: 0-936480-07-6 Student hard cover edition
ISBN: 0-936480-08-4 Teacher edition

Dedicated to the
Yokuts, the first people
of the Great Central Valley
of California

Dear Reader,

Before the coming of the Europeans, California was the home of 150,000 to 300,000 Indians! Of more than 100 different Indian tribes in California, the Yokuts tribe was the largest. It has been estimated that the Yokuts numbered no less than 25,000!

Yokuts land included all of the Great Central Valley of California. In this great valley there lived about 50 different tribes of Yokuts, each with its own name, territory, and dialect.

Each tribe spoke a dialect of the Yokuts main language. A dialect is a form of a main language with some changes in words, meanings, and pronunciations. Can you imagine 50 different dialects spoken in an area 350 miles long and 75 miles wide?

Many Yokuts tribes lived in the northern part of the Great Central Valley. Their territory stretched from the Sacramento River to what is today the city of Fresno. Here in the Northern Yokuts territory, the great San Joaquin River, teeming with salmon, sturgeon, and pike, wound its way through vast stretches of tules. Beyond the towering tules, huge oak trees provided great harvests of acorns.

On the western slopes of the Sierra Nevada foothills lived the Foothill Yokuts tribes. From the high snow-capped peaks of the Sierras, trout-filled streams flowed into the foothills. Oak trees dotted the hillsides and deer roamed throughout the pine forests.

The Yokuts tribes in the southern part of the Great

Central Valley lived in a vast territory reaching from the present day city of Fresno to the Tehachapi Mountains. A maze of rivers and lakes covered this low flat land. Tule choked sloughs and marshes brimmed with fish and sheltered huge flocks of ducks and geese. With their tule boats, the Southern Valley Yokuts used the rivers and marshes as waterways for travel.

Here in the southern part of the Great Central Valley begins the story of Pasquala, a Yokuts Indian girl. Near the western shore of Buena Vista Lake, a cluster of kawes, tule-matted homes, formed the village of Tulamniu where Pasquala was born. At the time of her birth in the early 1800's, Spanish missions were being built along the California coast and many of the coastal Indian tribes had been taken into the mission system. The mission padres planned to start missions among the Great Central Valley Yokuts, but the Yokuts strongly resisted the Spanish influence.

The story of Pasquala is considered a legend. Although there is no proof that this legend is true, a girl like Pasquala may have lived and the events that happened to her in this story could have actually taken place.

As you read Pasquala's story, let your imagination take you back in time to a thriving Indian village in the beautiful unspoiled land of California. Think about the Yokuts and a way of life that will always be a part of the whispers of California.

The Authors

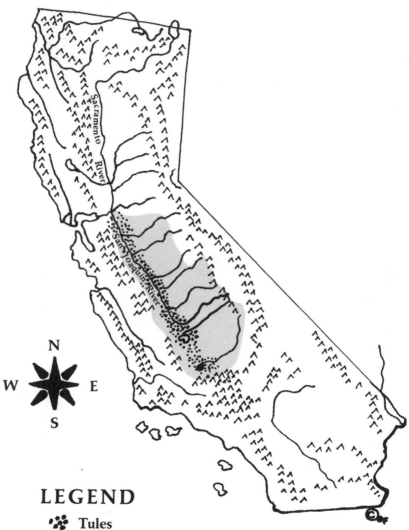

LEGEND

Tules

O Tulare Lake - former large lake

● Buena Vista Reservoir - former lake

Mountains

Rivers

Yokuts' Territory

TRIBES OF CALIFORNIA

Table of Contents

Chapter One

The Hiding Place

Mother and I stayed very still, crouching near the back wall of the cave. We had been hiding in the old cave for a long time and my arms and legs ached from sitting still for so long. The musty smell of the cave made me wrinkle my nose. Mother held her hand to my face warning me not to sneeze. Her look told me that we had to be very quiet. Without a sound, I stretched my legs and looked at the cave walls. Leaning forward, I stared at the lines painted on the wall. My eyes followed the path of the markings until I found the pictographs, the painted pictures on the cave walls. I knew I could not move to touch them as I had so many times before. Looking at the pictographs made me think about the times I had come to this cave with my mother and father and other Yokuts tribal members to watch special ceremonies. I remembered my father, an elder of the tribe, singing with the men singers. I would sit close to the singers listening to their voices and tapping my foot to the rhythm of the clapsticks. I remembered how I had listened for the footsteps of the dancers as they entered the cave in single file and how their feather skirts swayed back and forth when they moved their bare feet to the music. Suddenly a sound interrupted my thoughts. I knew I should be listening for the footsteps of strangers not the footsteps of dancers.

Silently, my mother moved in front of me. She turned her head and listened to the noise near the opening of the cave. The willow branches that covered the opening of the cave were slowly parted. In the dim light I could see the shape of a man bending down to enter our hiding place. A shiver ran through my body. Was this man a soldado from the mission far over the hills? Had he come to look for the Chumash Indians who had run away from the mission? I covered my eyes with my hands and turned away from the man. I pressed my body against the cold wall of the cave hoping the man wouldn't see me. A hand touched my shoulder. I opened my eyes, looked up, and there stood my father. He told us that we no longer had to stay hidden in the cave and that he had come to take us back to our village. The worried look left my mother's face. We were no longer afraid.

Stepping out of the dark cave, I shielded my eyes from the bright sunlight. Father told us that soldados had been seen that morning riding their large brown horses along the trail that led through the tall patches of tules. They were following the well-worn path along the shores of the lake leading to our village. The soldados were looking for Chumash Indians who had run away from the missions near the ocean. When the soldados entered our village, most of us were not in the village at that time. Many of our men had been fishing on the lake or were in the marshes setting nets for birds and ducks. I had been with mother and some of the other women and children on the shores of the lake cutting and gathering large bundles of tules. While we were working, mother looked up and saw puffs of smoke that were rising from an Indian village west of us. Mother yelled a warning that strangers were nearby. Mother and I had run from the marshes to the safety of the secret cave. Most of our people were too far from the cave, so they had hidden in the thick patches of tules. This was not the first time that strangers had come to our valley and we knew where to hide when we wanted to keep out of sight.

Walking back to our village, I knelt down in the path and traced my fingers around one of the hoofprints that had been left by the soldados' horses. I shuddered to think that the soldados had ridden their horses along this same path this very morning! Father showed us where he had hidden in a thick clump of tall tules not far from the path. Father had been so close to the leather-jacketed soldados that he could smell the sweat of their hard-ridden horses. Our hearts were glad that father had found a safe hiding place in the tules.

That evening everyone in our kawe, our large tule-matted home, gathered together and talked excitedly about the frightening soldados and why they had come. Lying on my tule mat, wrapped in my rabbit-skin blanket, I listened to the low murmur of the grown-up voices. The chief of our tribe said that more and more soldados were coming to our valley, but father said our hiding places were good and we would always be safe. The talking went on and on and I heard a new word— traders. Who were they? Would we have to hide from them when they came? The soft voices became a blur in my head. I could no longer keep my eyes open and soon I fell fast asleep on my tule mat.

Chapter Two

Men in Moccasins

The next morning when I awoke, I could hear voices through the thick tule walls of the kawe. My mother and father were talking about the traders who would soon visit our village. There was that word again—traders. I sat up and listened. Father was telling mother that he needed cedar wood to make a strong new bow to hunt the great tule elk. Father had spent many weeks making arrowshafts from the strong stalks of hala, a small bamboo plant, that grew along the river banks. He hoped to trade the hala arrowshafts for the prized cedar wood that the traders would bring. Mother was telling father about the foods that she and the other women of the village were preparing for the feast that would follow the trading.

Pushing aside the elk skin that covered the opening of our kawe, I stepped out into the morning light. I rubbed the sleep from my eyes. Puffs of smoke filled the sky. The signal fires again! I ran to my mother's side afraid that the soldados and their frightening horses were coming back to our village. Mother smiled at me and told me that these smoke signals were being sent from a nearby Yokuts' village. This time the smoke told us Shoshone traders not soldados were coming. The traders lived on the other side of the great mountains to the east of us. They were bringing goods to trade with many tribes of Yokuts who lived in the Great Valley of the Tules. Now, I knew what the word traders meant! Would there be many of them? Would they come on horses? What would they bring to trade?

Mother asked me to fill a small carrying basket with dried tule roots from the granary. As I walked to the granary where the roots were stored, I could feel excitement in the air as the women of our village prepared a feast that would be given for the traders when the trading was over. I passed women pounding acorns into meal. The thump, thump, thump of their heavy pestles echoed throughout the village. Young girls were filling baskets with seeds and dried meat. Others were heaping duck eggs in large baskets and making fires to cook fresh fish. The smell of roasting duck made my mouth water. As I passed a group of men, I heard them talking about the traders. I heard one of the men say he wanted to trade a stone wedge for the glass-like obsidian found in the mountains. I knew that obsidian made the best arrowheads and the men of our village depended upon traders to bring obsidian. Another group of men talked about trading for cedar wood to make new bows to hunt the great tule elk that roamed the valley floor. The best bow maker in our village talked about how bows made from cedar wood were very strong and lasted many years. All the men had selected their best stone tools, arrowshafts, and carved fish charms to trade for the obsidian and cedar wood. Everyone was talking about the traders. As I helped my mother pound the dried tule roots into meal, I too, began to feel the excitement of this day.

Before mother and I could finish pounding the tule roots, the chief's son came running into our village and told us that the traders were just below the river. With the village dogs yapping at our heels, I ran with the other children to meet the group of men who soon came on foot down the river trail. The six men were from the Shoshone tribe far to the east. The heavily-burdened Shoshones were bent under the weight of large net sacks filled with trade goods. Each man carried a large carved bow. Hung over each man's shoulder was a raccoon skin quiver filled with arrows. Obsidian blades and rabbit sticks were tied around

the men's waists with leather thongs. One of the men stopped to shift his heavy net sack. Getting up my courage, I moved close to the man. What was he wearing on his feet? He wasn't wearing tule sandals like my people, the Yokuts. I bent down and touched the soft deerskin moccasins that covered his feet. I wondered what it would be like to wear deerskin moccasins. I looked up into the face of the trader and he smiled at me.

The traders moved along the trail quickly. Running along beside them my short legs could hardly keep up with their long steps. Wearing a black and white feathered cape, our chief stepped forward to greet the visitors as they entered the village. My father and my uncle also stepped forward to take part in the greeting. I heard my uncle say to my father that he recognized some of these men. He had traded with them before and they had made good exchanges. My father knew the trading would go well.

Everyone followed the chief of our tribe to a special place where a ramada, an open-sided shelter, had been built that morning. In the cool shade of the ramada, the Shoshone traders sat down and spread out several deerskins. From their heavy packs they took out stone tools, pine nuts, obsidian, bracken fern roots, cedar wood, and many other trade goods.

My father and uncle sat down facing the traders. They spread out large elk skins. One by one, men from our tribe came forward with nets, carved stone fishing weights, soapstone beads, turtle shells, elk skins, and elk horns they wanted to trade. While the rest of the tribe watched, each man made his trade. The Shoshone traders and the men of our village did not understand each other's words so most of the trading was done with sign language. The children of the tribe crowded in closely behind their fathers and mothers to watch the trading. During the next several hours of trading even the smallest child was quiet. Only the scuffing of feet broke the silence when each man stepped forward to trade.

The men bargained with each other during the long afternoon. At last it was time for my father to trade. He laid four beautiful hala arrowshafts and his carved stone scraper on the skin. In exchange he selected a fine piece of cedar wood. Father was pleased to get the strong cedar wood limb from which he would make a new bow for hunting the great tule elk. As he looked at my mother, he noticed that she was looking at a large bundle of bracken fern roots. Father offered two more of his hala arrowshafts and the trader handed him the bundle of roots. A smile crossed mother's face for now she would be able to finish the beautiful basket she had started last winter.

I thought the trading had finally come to an end when the trader who had smiled at me earlier that day reached down into his net sack and took out a small pair of deerskin moccasins. Father took his last remaining arrowshafts and offered them to the trader for the moccasins. The trader shook his head and looked at me. I touched the abalone shell necklace I wore around my neck. He nodded. I lifted the necklace from my neck and placed it next to my father's arrowshafts. The trader looked at the necklace and arrowshafts in front of him. Would he accept the things my father and I had offered? Smiling at me, the trader picked up the moccasins and placed them in my hands. He put the arrowshafts and abalone shell necklace into his pack, rose to his feet, and motioning with his hands he declared that the trading was over.

Everyone shouted and laughed as the women in our tribe stepped forward and threw handfuls of chia seeds over the men who had traded during the warm, spring afternoon. Later, as the sun set behind the hills, the women brought baskets of baked tule roots, acorn mush, roasted fish, duck, and turtle meat. Feasting and admiring each other's new goods went on late into the evening.

When the evening grew cooler, we gathered close to the fires that glowed in the dark. Most of the men and women played guessing games over and over again. My favorite game was played with two bones. One bone was marked with a small piece of leather tied around it. Two teams sat facing each other. One player held a bone in each hand and would shuffle the bones from hand to hand. A player from the opposite team would try to guess which hand held the marked bone. My father was fast at shuffling the bones from one hand to the other and even though I watched his hands like a hawk, I could never guess in which hand he held the marked bone. Everyone would laugh and stamp their feet when he fooled the other team. The games went on late into the night. I could tell by the laughter of my people that they were happy with everything that had happened that day.

Early the next morning I followed the traders when they left our village and walked down the trail to the lake. As they moved past the willow trees near the lake, my friend the trader turned and waved at me. I wondered how long I would have to wait until the traders visited our village again.

Chapter Three

The Rattlesnake Basket

Spring rains kept us inside the kawe for several days following the traders' visit. Listening to the steady beat of the rain hitting against the thick tule walls of our kawe, I watched mother finish a rattlesnake basket that the Rattlesnake Doctor would soon use in a special ceremony. Mother knew a live rattlesnake would be put in the basket so she had woven the fibers extra tight.

I thought of the special place where mother and I had gathered the roots and grasses for this basket. We had used our digging sticks to unlace the tangled sedge roots that would be used to begin the basket. Mother had cleaned and stripped the roots and started the basket by twisting the root fibers into a small coil. Gradually, she had added different grasses to form a large basket with a rattlesnake pattern. She had used redbud bark to stitch red designs into the basket and bracken fern root to make black designs. Mother had worked each day weaving her basket and I had watched very

13

carefully for soon I would be making baskets. As mother stitched the diamond pattern of the rattlesnake around the curve of the basket, the pattern seemed to come alive with each row.

There had not been enough bracken fern root and mother had left the basket unfinished until the traders visited our village. The day after the traders had left, mother had buried the fern roots in tule swamp mud to dye them black.

Now, with her deer bone awl, mother used the black fern roots to stitch tiny pairs of ant figures around the narrow neck of the rattlesnake basket. Watching mother stitch the trails of black ants, made me think of a legend she had told me many times.

*   *   *

The Legend of the Ants
and the Rattlesnake

In the Yokuts' religion the rattlesnake is the private messenger of Tihpiknits, the keeper of the Indian Hereafter. The rattlesnake crawls about and spies on the Yokuts. When he finds a bad Yokuts, he sends the name to Tihpiknits who orders the death of the bad Yokuts.

Once a bad rattlesnake sent to Tihpiknits the names of some good people and they died. Quail learned what had been done

14

and told the water skater who can travel on land and water to carry the word to the ants. Hundreds and hundreds of ants marched into the land of the rattlesnakes. They found the bad rattlesnake, stung him to death, and ate him. The ants warned the rattlesnakes to be good to the Yokuts or they would return and destroy all of them.

From that time on, rattlesnake baskets have had ants or quail or water skater designs stitched on them to warn the rattlesnakes to be good to the Yokuts.

* * *

When the spring rains stopped and the sun warmed the land, the Rattlesnake Doctor started to prepare for the rattlesnake ceremony. This ceremony would keep our people safe from rattlesnake bites during the coming summer when everyone would be in the fields gathering seeds and berries.

The Rattlesnake Doctor and a helper went to a rock pile where the snakes lived. With sticks they caught several large rattlesnakes and put them into baskets. The day of the ceremony the Rattlesnake Doctor painted white and red stripes on his face and body. He took mother's basket, lined it with soft eagle down, and put it into a hole he had dug in the ground. The other children and I stood watching as the Rattlesnake Doctor picked the largest rattlesnake and put it into mother's basket. He used a stick to coax the viper into the narrow neck of the basket. The movement of the snake's body frightened me and again I noticed how perfectly my mother had copied the snake's diamond pattern onto her basket.

Late in the afternoon everyone gathered to take part in the ceremony. The Rattlesnake Doctor did a one-step dance in time to the voices of the singers. Soon the Rattlesnake Doctor took the snake out of the basket. Holding the snake in his hands, he danced among the people, lifting the snake over everyone's heads. Then he put the snake back into the basket. The people danced around in a circle in front of the basket and each person held one bare foot over the rattlesnake in the basket. My parents held me by the hand and led me into the circle. I was shaking as I put my foot over mother's beautiful basket.

When I lifted my foot away from the basket, I breathed a deep sigh and stepped back quickly. The snake hadn't bitten me! It did not bite anyone! Our Rattlesnake Doctor said that it was his powerful magic that had protected all of us from the rattlesnake, but I knew the ants that mother had woven on her basket had told the rattlesnake to be good to the Yokuts.

Chapter Four

Thunder in the Earth

Early that summer I took my first trip to the seashore. I was eight summers old. Many of the people in our village made the annual trip to the ocean to collect and dry enough shellfish to last our village for one year.

The night before we left on our journey, everyone was busy packing supplies. It would be a long trip to the seashore and everyone had to help carry his own share. The women packed belongings and food into large cone-shaped burden baskets. I helped my mother fill her basket with loop sticks, stirring paddles, digging sticks, small baskets, skins for bedding, seeds, acorn and tule meal. When we finished, mother's basket was filled to the top. I watched father as he packed his carrying net. He selected his best obsidian blades, bone hooks, stone tools, fishing weights, small nets, and drilling sticks for starting cooking fires. I helped him tie the net closed. Before we went to sleep that night, father gave me a small leather pouch with a long strap.

It was filled with seeds and pieces of dried meat and was my very own carrying pouch!

The next morning, father helped mother lift the heavily-loaded burden basket filled with our belongings onto her back. Father slipped one end of a strong woven tumpline around her basket and the other end of the tumpline over mother's forehead. Mother wore a brimless basket cap on her head to protect her forehead from the pull of the scratchy tumpline. Father lifted his heavy net onto his back and tied it with a strap around his chest. He carried his cedar bow and raccoon skin quiver over his shoulder. Mother and father wore tule sandals, but I wore my deerskin moccasins. I hung my pouch over my shoulder and together the three of us joined the other people of our tribe to start our long journey to the seashore. Father said it would take six days and nights to reach the ocean. He said we would leave our village by the lake and travel westward through many hills and valleys.

Our group started happily along the trail that led west to the mountain passes. Several of the village dogs followed close at our heels yipping and barking excitedly. They raced ahead and then ran back to us as if to tell us to hurry along. The dogs seemed as eager to go to the seashore as we were.

As we traveled westward across the marshlands

and down the sloughs thick with tules, we could see great herds of brown tule elk in the distance. Our footsteps disturbed many birds and great flocks of red-winged blackbirds flew up from the marshes darkening the skies over our heads. Walking single file, our group moved swiftly across the valley and into the first range of hills. Moving up into the rolling hills, we left the heavy heat of the valley behind us.

As we looked back into the valley below, we could see the vast green and brown patches of tules that covered the valley floor. Father pointed to our little village near the shores of the great blue lake. We could see wisps of smoke rising from the cooking fires in our village. Far, far to the east, we could see the tall mountains with the last patches of snow clinging to their highest peaks.

We wound our way upward and over the range of hills. Late that afternoon we came down through a pass in the hills to a valley. We camped near the mouth of a river and father said that we would follow this river for the next few days. By the time I had awakened the next morning, the men had speared trout and the women had gathered baskets of watercress for our meal.

That day as we followed the river, we passed through groves of oak trees where our tribe gathered acorns in the fall. Golden flowers bloomed along the river banks and clouds cast dark shadows on the mountains in front of us. In the next few days we would be climbing those tall mountains covered with pine forests. That night we camped in an abandoned Chumash village. Mother told me that when the Chumash had lived in this valley we would not have come into their territory without their permission. We would have followed another trail to the sea. There was sadness in my heart as I wondered why the Chumash people had left this beautiful valley.

Several days later we climbed the path into the pine forests. Never before had I smelled the fragrance of the pine trees. I was used to the smell of the marshes and sloughs in the Valley of the Tules. As we walked swiftly along the trail, I heard the scolding of the blue jays in the pines. I wanted to chase the chipmunks as they scurried up and down the tree trunks, but mother warned me to stay on the path close by her side. There was the danger of bears in the pine forest and I noticed that other children in the group stayed close to the adults.

Each day as the sun disappeared behind the mountains and the day slowly darkened into night, our group would find a place to rest. Several cook fires were started and women would prepare the evening meal for the men, women, and children who had come on the trip. After sharing the meal, the women and children gathered pine needles to make beds to sleep upon.

One evening after we had finished a light meal of dried meat and chia seeds, my father told us that it would be two more days of hard travel before we reached the seashore.

The next morning as we climbed higher into the pine forests, I noticed that the chipmunks had disappeared and the chatter of the blue jays could no longer be heard. The dogs that had come with us on the trip began to whine and whimper. Suddenly, the ground began to shake as if a thunderstorm was raging deep down inside the center of the earth. The earth shook and it seemed as if the ground was about to split open. Right in front of us, an old pine tree trembled and began to sway slowly back and forth. I stood frozen, unable to move as the large tree started to give way. Mother snatched me by the arm and pulled me off the path as the pine tree crashed to the ground. The noise of the pine tree's crash echoed back and forth in the canyons below us. The ground gave one last great shake as the thundering noise inside the earth died away. Then all was quiet.

A loud shout from one of the men at the head of the group took us running to look at a giant crack in the earth. I clung to my father's side as we stood looking down into the deep opening in the ground. Would I be able to see the center of the earth where the thunderstorm had raged? All I could see was darkness far down in the crack.

The men and women looked at each other and an elder of the tribe motioned with his hand that everyone should sit down. No one spoke. We waited until the sun was straight overhead and then the elder motioned that we would continue our journey. We gathered our baskets and packs and started again on our journey to the sea.

Chapter Five

The Great Blue Ocean

On the final day of our journey to the sea, we crossed the last range of mountains. Far down the trail, we caught our first glimpse of the great blue ocean. Everyone stopped to gaze upon the vast ocean below us. I stared at the water sparkling in the sunlight as the waves rolled in to touch the golden strip of sand. The water crashing against the rocks sounded like mean Pú-Muk, the thunder maker, smashing things and making big thunder. Cool ocean breezes brought us the smell of seaweed and all of us could taste salt when we licked our lips.

As we followed the path down to the ocean, I became more and more excited. When we finally reached the beach, I ran toward the water. My feet sank into the cool, soft sand. The water rushed toward me and as I turned to run away, I felt the sand swirling under my feet. The foamy water splashed against my legs and almost knocked me over. Suddenly, the water slipped back into the sea

and there I stood with my feet buried in the sand. As far as I could see there was nothing but beautiful blue water.

We camped in a protected area near the seashore where we spent the next few weeks fishing and gathering shellfish. I liked helping mother and the other women gather the glistening shellfish from the large rocks on the beach. When the waves swept out to sea, the men used their blades to scrape abalone, mussels, barnacles, and turban snails from the rocks. I filled a small basket with the shellfish and raced back to high ground just before the waves came crashing back against the rocks. The men went into the deeper waters and netted rockfish. Many times I watched them drag nets filled with shimmering fish onto the beach. I helped the women clean the fish and then the fish were dried over low fires. Many days went by before the fish were dry enough to be packed into burden baskets. Soon we would carry the baskets back to our village.

One morning when the tide was out farther than usual, the women and children went down to the beach to gather seaweed from the rocks. Because the tide was so far out, we walked on the rocky floor of the ocean. In the distance we could hear the pounding and crashing of the angry ocean waves. Mother told me that we had to move quickly across the rocks because soon the tide would come back and cover the rocks where we stood.

Pools of water had been left behind as the tide went out and in these tide pools I saw pink crabs and tiny fish. In some of the small pools sea anemones and sea urchins blossomed like flowers. What fun it was to drop tiny pebbles onto these creatures and watch them quickly close their long tentacles.

As we collected seaweed into baskets and nets, the women and children began to spread out among the tide pools and rocks and move away from the shore. For awhile, I stayed with the others and then I found myself following a long tide pool that seemed to have no end. I looked down into the tide pool and saw colorful sea slugs, tiny, shiny fish darting about, and giant chitons that clung to the sides of the rocks. I reached into the tide pool and the clear water suddenly turned dark. It was a baby octopus spurting its ink so I couldn't see it. The octopus had been trapped in the tide pool when the tide had moved out to sea. I knelt by the pool waiting for the water to clear so I could catch the octopus.

Suddenly, I heard the roar of the ocean and water splashed against my legs. I jumped up and saw that the ocean waves were quickly beginning to come back to shore. The tide pool I had been following had led me far, far from the beach and I knew I had to get back to shore. Running as fast as I could toward the beach, the water rose higher and higher. I jumped from rock to rock. Gasping for breath, I reached safety. I turned and saw that the rocks and tide pools were gone! They were covered by the swirling ocean waters.

After several weeks the time had come for our return trip to our valley. The evening before we left, a great feast was held to celebrate our good catch of fish. The women prepared baskets of fish for everyone to enjoy. I ate fish and shellfish that I had not tasted before. Mother showed me how to bite off the tip and sip the juices from the horn snails she gave me. We tossed the empty shells onto a shell mound. I kept the prettiest shells in my carrying pouch. My shells would always remind me of my first trip to the great blue ocean.

Chapter Six

A Decision Is Made

The morning we were to leave on the return trip to our village, I became ill. My stomach ached and my head was hot with fever. My mother gave me tea made with herbs that she had carried with her on our long journey. We started homeward on the trail with our people, but I became so sick that my mother and father feared I would die. My parents had heard of the padres at Santa Inés Mission and as our fishing group came through the valley close to the mission, my parents decided not to continue the journey home. My father carried me in his arms to the mission to ask the padres for help.

Entering the mission grounds, we met a padre who led us down a long corridor and into a small room. The padre motioned to my father to put me on a narrow cot. The padre leaned over me and softly spoke some words which I didn't understand. He stood by my side and put his cool hand on my burning forehead. Soon another padre appeared who knew a few words of our language. My father and mother told the padre that we were Yokuts from the Valley of the Tules, a long journey through the mountain passes east of the mission. They told how we had come to the seashore with many members of our tribe to gather and dry fish to be taken back to our village. They told the padre that on the last day of our fishing trip, we had had a great feast and this morning I had become very ill. The padre smiled and nodded his head. He left the room and in a while he returned with a small bowl of clear soup. He lifted my head and slowly spooned some of the soup into my mouth. I swallowed some of it. I did not like the taste.

Lying on the cot, my stomach ached and my head was hot. It was hard to keep my eyes open. Mother stood by the side of my cot and held my hand. I could hear my father's low voice speaking to me, but I was too weak to answer him. I was very tired and soon I fell asleep.

During the days when I was sick, my mother and father helped the padres with the work at the mission. My parents told me that they had met many Chumash Indians living at the mission, but there were only a few Indians from the Valley of the Tules.

As I grew stronger, I was able to walk about the mission. I asked my mother if there were soldados living at this mission. I had always feared the soldados and even though I had never seen one, I had heard many terrible stories about them. Mother told me that only a few soldados lived at Mission Santa Inés. She said that most of the soldados lived in a fort over the mountain range south of us. Mother told me a story she had heard from an Indian woman at the mission. The woman's brother had tried to run away from the mission and had been caught by the soldados and whipped. When he ran away again, the soldados caught him and locked him in a cell for many weeks. Mother warned me not to go near the soldados and told me that as long as we were here at Santa Inés Mission we were to follow the padres' rules.

My parents talked about leaving Mission Santa Inés and returning to our village. We knew that we should not stay at the mission. Father had always told me we were not to leave our village and live a different way of life. Father had said that when the Yokuts followed the ways of their people there was always peace and happiness. We knew that if we stayed at the mission, we would be breaking the ways of our tribe. We would bring unhappiness to ourselves and to our people.

One evening, as my parents spoke quietly about

leaving the mission, I heard my father say that if we did not leave soon he would be too ashamed to go home. The soldados also worried my father. Would they be sent after us if we left the mission? I could tell by the sound of my parents' voices that their hearts were heavy wondering if we should stay at the mission or return to our village. What would the padres do if we left? Would the people of our village understand why we had come to the mission?

When several weeks had passed, the padre asked us to be baptized. He told us that baptism meant we would become neophytes, new members, of the Christian church. We would follow the rules of the church and live and work at the mission. The mission would give us food, clothing, and blankets and at certain times, we would be allowed to visit our village.

After listening to the padre, my father knew a decision had to be made. I remember the troubled look in my father's eyes. Father knew he was in disgrace with our people because he had left the tribe and was living at the mission. He didn't want to go home to the unhappiness he had caused the people of our village. He decided that we would be baptized and live at the mission.

In the next few months, the padre taught us

about the Christian God. When the padre baptized us, he chose the name José for my father and the name María for my mother. He gave me the name of Pasquala and told me it meant "one who loves and helps others." Our lives as neophytes at Mission Santa Inés had begun.

Chapter Seven

A Different Way of Life

The ringing of the mission bells at sunrise began our day. After prayers, the bells called us to our morning meal. We no longer ate thick acorn meal mush, but were given atolé, a thin mush made of cornmeal or barley. Sometimes vegetables were added to the atolé. When the sun was straight over head, our work-filled mornings ended with another bowl of atolé that sometimes had meat added to it. At the end of the long hot afternoons the bells called us to evening prayers and the evening meal. After the meal, the padres handed us pieces of fruit grown in the mission orchards. The neophytes had planted young fruit trees in straight rows close to the mission walls. During the warm months, the tree branches bent under the weight of purple figs and golden peaches. My favorite fruit was the size of my fist. Round and red with a tough skin, this fruit was filled with red seeds. I loved chewing the seeds as they stained my fingers and lips with their juicy sweetness. It was hard for me to say the name of this fruit. Pom-e-gran-ate!

At the mission, the padres would not allow my mother and me to wear tule skirts. We wore long dresses that touched our ankles. I did not like the way the skirt scratched my legs and felt heavy on my body. My father wore a woolen shirt that reached to his knees. He also wore a breechcloth or long pants. It took me awhile to get used to seeing my parents in their strange clothes.

The padres spoke a language different from ours. Most of the neophytes at the mission spoke the Chumash language and the language of the padres. One of the padres spoke a few words of the Yokuts language. He told us stories about his God. He also taught us to speak the Spanish language.

I missed speaking my own language and I missed hearing the Yokuts stories that my grandfather had told me. I'll always remember sitting around the warm fire in our kawe on long winter evenings, listening to the stories that grandfather had told. When Wátihte, the ground owl would call, grandfather would then tell the story of Tihpiknits, the Great Bird Person, and Ki-yu, the Coyote. I know it best of all my stories.

*   *   *

The Legend of Tihpiknits and Ki-yu

Tihpiknits is the name of the Great Bird Person who rules over the Yokuts' Land of the Dead. Tihpiknits' Pahn is the land where the dead Indians go. It is six nights journey to the north. Only the good people can get there. The dead people dance a Lonewis or crying dance there every night. They play games and have a good time. They eat Toi-uk, a food, that never gets any smaller, no matter how much they eat. In the morning the dead all disappear and nothing can be seen of them until the next night when Winatun, the messenger, builds new fires for the dancers and calls them all back. The Yokuts always walk quietly through the forest for it may be the place where the dead hold their Lonewis.

In Tihpiknits' Pahn, Ki-yu, the Coyote, and Tihpiknits, the Great Bird Person, always play the old game of Hih-sa Na-us. When Tihpiknits wins, one of the Yokuts must die and go to Tihpiknits' Pahn. When Ki-yu wins, he tries to bite Tihpiknits and pulls feathers from him. Ki-yu throws the feathers that he pulls from Tihpiknits to the south and the north wind brings them to the Yokuts in the form of the first white geese of the winter. When the Yokuts see the first white geese come they know Ki-yu, the Coyote, won the game. When the Yokuts hear Wátihte, Tihpiknits' messenger, wail in the evening, they know Tihpiknits, the Great Bird Person, has won the game and that someone who has died is arriving in Tihpiknits' Pahn to dance in the Lonewis forever.

* * *

In the springtime, father helped the other men at the mission shear the wool from the sheep. They carried the wool to the mission workshops where mother and I spent most of our time. I helped remove burrs, sticks, and thorns from the wool. Then the wool was washed in large kettles and spread on bushes to dry. When the wool was dry, the women pulled it over brushes made of spiny teasel pods. The spiny teasel combed the knots and tangles out of the wool and straightened the fibers. With a drop spindle, I learned to spin the fibers into long strands of yarn. I carried the yarn to my mother who sat at a large loom. How swiftly her fingers moved as she wove the strands of yarn into pieces of cloth that would be made into clothing for the neophytes.

Late in the afternoon, some of the boys would leave the workshops and go to the church for choir practice. When I asked the padre if I could sing with the choir, he told me that only boys were allowed to join the choir. Sometimes when the padre wasn't looking, I would slip into the back of the church, sit quietly in the corner, and listen to the beautiful voices.

One day the padre saw me in the back of the church and motioned for me to come forward. He pointed to a large music book that lay on a wooden stand facing the choir. I looked at the large book with the colored notes while the padre pointed to each note with his stick. I noticed that as the notes on the page moved up the lines, so did the voices in the boys' choir. As the notes moved down the lines, the voices went down. When the padre's stick pointed to the last note on the page, he motioned for me to turn to the next page of the music book. My eyes soon began to follow the notes and as the singers' voices moved up and down, I found that I could follow the notes and turn the pages of the book without the padre giving me directions. From that time, I always turned the pages of the music book for the choir. Although I was not allowed to sing in the boys' choir, I was happy to be part of the beautiful music.

As the days went by, I thought about my small village on the shores of the lake in the tules. How different my life was now. Mother no longer gathered tules, father no longer hunted the great tule elk, and I no longer ran free to look for wild duck eggs or search for turtles. My heart longed for my people that lived far over the mountains in the Valley of the Tules.

Chapter Eight

Visitors

When one summer had passed, a messenger from our people came to Mission Santa Inés to speak to my father. He had been sent by the chief and the elders of our tribe. The messenger told my father that the people of our tribe were not happy that we were living at the mission. They wanted us to return to the Valley of the Tules. These words disturbed my father, but we did not leave the mission. Messengers came to the mission whenever the Yokuts traveled through the mountain passes on the way to the great blue ocean. After a time, the messengers no longer came. I wondered if our people still kept us in their hearts.

By the time I was twelve summers old, my mother had taught me to weave. Now, instead of spinning wool with a drop spindle, I worked at a large loom like my mother. With a wooden shuttle, I wove long strands of yarn back and forth across the loom to make wide pieces of cloth. At the end of the day I piled the pieces of cloth I had woven near the doorway of the workshop. Another neophyte would take the cloth to the sewing room where clothing was made for the people at the mission.

Each day as we worked, the padre brought us a clay jar of cool water. One day the padre asked us to share the water with the workers in the leather shop where my father made saddles. Mother and I left our weaving and started down the corridor. When we reached the far side of the corridor near the leather shop, we saw my father talking with two soldados. The soldados were looking at a beautiful leather saddle that my father was finishing. As my mother and I moved closer, I could see my father's hands slowly tooling a design on the sides of the saddle horn. How carefully my father moved the blade into the soft material, pushing the leather into beautiful curves and shapes. The leaf-like designs reminded me of the grapevines that grew in the mission vineyards.

As the soldados watched my father tooling the design on the saddle, I heard them say that they had come from the presidio in Santa Barbara. One soldado began to move about the workshop talking to the neophytes as they worked. The other soldado leaned heavily against my father's workbench. Each time he tried to talk, he coughed. When he saw the water jar that my mother and I had brought, he pushed the wide brimmed black hat he wore back from his face and motioned for me to bring him a cup of water. As he drank the water, I noticed how tired he looked. Waiting for him to finish, I looked at him carefully. Over a long sleeved shirt, he wore a cuera, a vest made of many layers of leather, and a shoulder belt that held bullets. There were burrs and dry leaves clinging to his dark wool pants. When the soldado stepped from behind the workbench to fill his cup again, I saw his high leather boots and heard the jangle of the large spiked rowels on his spurs. Finishing his drink, he passed the cup back to me and I refilled the cup for my father.

While my mother and I were passing the cool water to the other neophytes in the workshop, the padre appeared. After talking with the soldados, he told my father and the other workers that the soldados at the presidio needed saddles. The padre wanted my father and the others to go with the soldados to Santa Barbara to deliver the leather goods.

The next morning I watched my father harness a mule to a carreta, a small cart, and load the carreta with saddles. He covered the saddles with a heavy wool blanket to protect them from the dust

and hot sun. Driving the carreta, father followed the soldados on their horses through the mission gates. Four neophytes from the mission joined the group as they started down the long trail to Santa Barbara. I waved to my father until I could only see puffs of dust in the far distance. I knew my father would not return for many days and I would miss him.

During the time my father was away, my mother and I continued our daily work. The days seemed longer with my father gone. Each morning before I went to the workshop, I stood at the mission gates looking down the trail hoping to see the men return. I could hardly wait to see my father and hear the story he would tell about his trip to Santa Barbara.

One morning as I stood at the mission gates, I heard people shouting from one of the storehouses. As I ran back to the mission courtyard, the padre raced past me pulling his gray robes up to his knees so he could run faster. Right behind him came four angry cooks waving large spoons and knives in the air. They yelled that a black bear was in the storehouse! I followed the padre and the cooks hoping to see the bear. When we reached the storehouse, we saw that the door had been smashed open. Large sacks of dried apples and apricots and a barrel of corn had been pulled outside and ripped open. A trail of dried beef led us down the hillside to the place where hundreds of red ladrillos, floor tiles, were drying in the sun. The padre pointed to several wet tiles with large bear pawprints in them. Everyone stopped running and looked at each other. We could see the bear's trail leading into a grove of trees. No one wanted to follow the bear into the forest! Laughing, all of us returned to the mission. Now, I had a story to tell my father when he returned from Santa Barbara!

Chapter Nine

A Time of Sadness

Late one evening the padre came to tell my mother that my father and the other neophytes had returned from Santa Barbara. The padre told her that the men had returned very tired and sick. The padre had taken them to the infirmary, the sickroom, and he told us we could not visit my father until morning.

When the first pink light of day brightened the sky, my mother and I went to the infirmary to see my father. The padre would not let us go into the sickroom. He told us that the men were very ill and we could see them from the doorway. As I peered into the darkened room, I could hear coughing and smell the strong scent of the tea that the padre brought to the sick men. Father was lying on a cot close to the door, a blanket tucked loosely around him. He was very quiet.

Later that morning when my mother and I returned to the infirmary and looked through the doorway, we could see my father tossing and

turning on his cot. His face, neck, and arms were covered with a red rash. While we stood at the door, a woman who was helping the padre care for the sick men told us that my father was very ill. Hearing our voices, my father opened his eyes and looked at us. When the woman left the room to get more water, father told us in a shaky voice that he was going to die. He asked us to leave the mission and return to the Valley of the Tules. Before we could speak to him, the woman returned and told us to leave the sickroom. As we walked out of the infirmary and down the corridor, tears filled our eyes. We knew that father was dying.

Five nights later my father died. My mother and I were sad and afraid. A few days after my father's death, three of the neophytes who had traveled to Santa Barbara with my father died. Fear spread throughout the mission. Although the padre worked day and night to care for the sick people, more and more neophytes became ill and died. Many of the workers in the shops stopped working. Mother and I knew that it was time to do what my father had told us. We had to leave the mission.

The next morning when the mission bells called us to prayers, mother told me that we were going to leave the mission and return to our valley. When the people at the mission went to the chapel, my mother gathered a few of our belongings and together we started off through the mountain passes to our home in the Valley of the Tules. We walked together in silence thinking about my father. What would become of us? Would the Yokuts welcome us back to our village?

The journey seemed long and slow. We followed a trail that I had never traveled before. Mother told me it was an old trail she had known as a child. It was longer, but easier with few high mountains to cross. Along the trail we picked berries and drank water from the mountain streams. At night we looked for shelter in caves or slept under a tree. As the trail came closer to the valley we could feel the warmth of the air that was rising from the hot valley floor.

Several days later we reached our village and went to my uncle's kawe. Mother told my uncle that my father had died at the mission. She said we had come home to the Valley of the Tules. My uncle did not say a word. He sat very still staring at us. My mother then tried to explain why we had gone to the mission. She said that my father had talked about returning to our village, but he knew he had disgraced his people. His feelings had kept him from returning to the Valley of the Tules. His last wish before he died was for us to come home where we belonged.

When my mother finished talking, there was a long silence and then my uncle spoke. He told mother and me that our family should have come back to the village long ago. My uncle's voice was stern when he told us the mission way of life was not our way of life. He said that by not returning to our village, we had weakened the spirit of our tribe. We were not living as our ancestors had taught us. My uncle told us he was unhappy with us and that we must never again leave our valley.

That night as I lay on my tule mat in my uncles' kawe, I thought about the death of my father. I began to cry softly. I could hear my mother crying, too. I knew she cried not only for the loss of my father, but for the sorrow that we had caused our people.

Chapter Ten

Like Stones in a Basket

At the first gray streaks of light, I awoke. I realized I had not heard the mission bells at dawn. For a moment I did not know where I was. Then the familiar sounds of the village came to my ears and I remembered what had happened to my father. I was home where I had wanted to be, but I had no feelings of happiness. When I looked at mother, she was awake. She stood and put her arm around me. Together we lifted the elk skin that covered the opening of the kawe and stepped into the busy life of the village.

The women of the village stared at us as they went about their morning work. They whispered to each other and motioned with their hands for us to come closer. They asked us why we had stayed at the mission. When my mother explained that I had been ill and the padres at Mission Santa Inés had helped me get better, the women looked at us as if they did not believe our story.

Mother and I tried to tell them that after I

recovered from my illness, we could not leave the mission for fear that the soldados would follow us to the village. No matter what we said, the people of our village only remembered that we had abandoned our duties as members of our tribe.

Without my father, loneliness filled our days and our nights. To show our love for him and to mourn his death as is the Yokuts' custom, mother and I put pitch and charcoal on our faces. When my uncle saw us, he asked that we wash away the pitch and charcoal and told us that no one should mourn someone who had brought disgrace to the tribe. The next day, even though we knew my uncle would be very angry, mother singed off our long black hair with a burning stick to show that we mourned father's death. When my uncle looked at us, anger flared in his eyes. Our close cropped hair reminded him of how we had gone against his wishes.

My uncle had given us the task of preparing each morning's meal for the people of our kawe. Every morning my mother and I awakened before dawn. We went alone to the granaries and filled our baskets with dry acorns. After removing the shells and winnowing the thin skins from the acorns, we sat at the grinding rocks pounding the nuts into a coarse meal. Before we could cook the acorn meal, we had to remove the bitter tasting tannic acid. We went to the stream where we dug holes in the sand and lined the holes with leaves. Then we spread acorn meal on top of the leaves. We covered the meal with more leaves and water was poured gently over the layers until the bitter tannic acid was washed away.

When the acorn meal was ready, I mixed it with water in a watertight basket while my mother used her loopstick to take hot stones from the fire. Mother carefully put the hot stones into the basket to cook the acorn meal and water into a mush. Again and again I stirred the mush to keep the stones from burning the bottom of the basket. As soon as the mush thickened and the nutlike smell filled the air, we knew the mush was warm and ready to eat. Mother removed the stones with her loopstick and set them aside in an empty basket. As I stared at the stones in the basket, I thought of my mother and myself. We worked hard at our jobs and then, like the cooking stones, we were put aside until we were needed again. Mother told me it would take time for my uncle and the people of our village to accept us again as members of the tribe. We were willing to work hard to prove to our people that we no longer had to be set aside like stones in a basket.

Chapter Eleven

Where the Tules Grew

For the next four summers we lived with my uncle, his wife, and four other families in a large kawe. Mother and I spent the days working with the other families. People were friendlier to us, but the stern looks from my uncle still made us feel sad and lonely.

Day after day, we walked the narrow trails to the marshes. Edging our way down the muddy path, the smell of the marshes and sloughs reminded me of the days long ago when I was a child. As we came to the thick green tules, we could see the black clouds of mosquitoes and hear their high pitched whine. We waded knee-deep into the marsh and with obsidian blades we slashed armloads of tules. We piled the tules on the shore. Later the men would tie the tules into bundles and make boat-like rafts. They would steer the tule boats through the sloughs and marshes spearing fish and searching for duck eggs and turtles.

Sometimes, mother and I would sit in the shade

near the marshes and weave the tule reeds into thick mats. We used these mats to repair the thatching on our kawe and granaries. My mother showed me how to weave a skirt from the tule reeds and how to pound tule fibers into soft linings for baby cradles. I learned to weave the tule fiber into rope and string that the men used for nets and traps.

Each day before we left the marshes, we dug tule roots from the shallow waters of the lake and spread them to dry in the sun. One day as I filled my basket with roots, I thought of my father and how much I missed him. I thought of the times he had been with us in the tules when we had gone to look for speckled duck eggs. His keen eyes had always spied the duck nests hidden in the tall tules. Together we had found the tracks of raccoons and antelope patterned in the mud. One day we followed the tracks of the tule elk. Father and I stood whisper-still looking across the marshes. A herd of tule elk stirred and slowly got up from their afternoon naps. As the elk grazed they edged away from us until all that we could see were their great racks of horns drifting along above the tules. Father had lifted me up on his shoulders so I had a better view and I watched until the last elk disappeared into the tall, green tules.

My thoughts were interrupted by a flash of red.

Red-winged blackbirds had swooped down in front of me to snap up a black cloud of mosquitoes. The tall slender tules swayed and bent under the weight of the birds, their wings beating rapidly as their beaks bobbed back and forth picking at the mosquitoes. Then as suddenly as the birds had come, they were gone, rising quickly above the tules into the clear blue sky. Stillness closed in around me. The tules loomed above my head and heat rising from the watery marshes hung in the air like cobwebs. Suddenly from the thick undergrowth, came the noisy croak of a bullfrog. It made me laugh out loud, but did not seem to disturb the great blue heron standing on stick-like legs waiting patiently to catch his dinner.

Parting the tules, I stepped out onto the shore of the lake. A family of ducks swam close to the water's edge. As I watched, the mother and father led their line of ducklings toward the middle of the lake leaving a trail of ripples behind them. As the ducks disappeared across the lake, I thought of my own family.

Turning, I saw my mother coming up the path lugging her heavy basket of tule roots. She motioned for me to come. Her hand felt good across my shoulders as I fell into step with her and together we carried our baskets of roots back to the village. It was good to be home with our people.

Chapter Twelve

Blackberries

When summer returned, my uncle and most of the members of our tribe made the trip to the seashore. My uncle did not ask us to go with him to the ocean. Mother and I stayed in the village with the older people, the chief, and the camp guards.

My uncle had given us permission to gather wild blackberries while he was away, but he told us we must go with some of the women who had remained in the village. I helped mother twine blackberry chawits, small baskets, made from the fiber of hemp and milkweed. We attached long fiber straps to each basket so each of us could hang a basket around our necks when we picked berries.

When the blackberries were ripe we left our village each morning and walked to the banks of the big river. We followed the trail through the cottonwood and willow trees growing along the river bank. As we came closer to the blackberry bushes flocks of ravens, blue jays, and magpies flew to the tops of the trees, where they perched and clamored at us as if to tell us to stay away from their berries.

Blackberry vines covered the ground like a thick blanket. Some of the blackberry bushes had wrapped themselves around the trunks of the trees and the vines hung down heavy with berries. Before we began to pick the berries, I tossed large rocks into the bushes. I wanted to warn the rattlesnakes that I was close by.

Each of us hung a blackberry basket around her neck so that our hands were free to pick the berries. Some of the women stepped carefully into the prickly bushes and used hook sticks to pull the berry vines close to them. The vines were so full that it did not take us long to fill our baskets. Filling the basket was easy, but filling my mouth with the sweet berries was more fun.

Each day we returned to the blackberry patch and filled our chawits. One afternoon mother signaled to me that the women's baskets were full and they were returning to the village. As I raced to join the group, my basket overturned and berries scattered all over the ground. Kneeling to pick up the berries, I heard the snap of dry twigs. My body froze at the sound. It was a sound I had heard before. I listened carefully. The bushes shook. There was a soft chewing sound. Rising slowly to my feet,

I looked across the top of the berry bushes. There in front of me was a huge brown bear. His back was to me. Sensing my closeness, he stood up on his hind legs, swung around, and stared right at me. Grabbing the chawit from around my neck, I hurled it at the huge bear. I turned and raced down the trail. Glancing back over my shoulder, I saw the large furry bear slobbering up my morning's work.

By the time I returned to the village, mother had mashed most of the berries she had picked that day. As she poured a thick layer of the mashed fruit into a flat basket to dry, she looked at me. Seeing the frightened look on my face, she didn't ask me about my missing berry basket, but listened to every word of my story. When I had finished telling about the bear, mother said that it was a wise thing I had acted so quickly. She told me it was better to meet a brown bear than a grizzly bear, the most dangerous of all bears. Mother laughed and told me she was glad I left the berries with the bear and had not let him follow me back to the village.

Several weeks later, mother took the thick slabs of dried blackberries, broke them into pieces, and stored them in baskets. The baskets were hung on the inside of our kawe. Every time I looked at the filled baskets, I thought of the huge brown bear that had liked the berries better than he had liked me!

Chapter Thirteen

The Salt Gatherers

In the heat of the summer, my uncle surprised mother and me by telling us that we could join the people in our village on the journey to the salt grass fields. We would travel north through the tules to the fields where our tribe had gathered salt grass for hundreds and hundreds of years.

The next day, before streaks of red had colored the eastern sky, we began our journey to the salt fields. As we followed the trail around the lake, we came to a campsite. The people of our village had used this campsite last spring when the great river that flowed from the mountains east of us had poured into our lake. The rushing water from the great river had caused the waters of our lake to rise. Flood waters had threatened our village and we had quickly gathered some belongings and moved to this higher campsite. When the waters went down, we moved back to our village. At other times, angry winds from the north blew the waters of the lake toward our village forcing my people to move once again to the higher campsite. Our camp guards were always alert and warned us when the waters of the lake began to rise.

Walking past the abandoned campsite, I noticed that the dry tules surrounding the lake had turned a light tan and hid the green tules that grew in the water. The vast patches of dry tules stretched as far as my eyes could see. Their light tan color matched the color of the animals living in the marshes. Moving quietly along the trail, we passed several young antelope that stood looking at us with their large black eyes. They were almost invisible against the tan background of the tules.

As the late afternoon sun faded and dropped below the horizon, we arrived at the salt grass fields. While setting up camp, I heard the scampering of small animals. Squinting my eyes, I could barely see the bodies of hundreds and hundreds of jackrabbits as they blended with the grasses and tules. When the evening cook fires were lit, shiny pairs of eyes stared at us from the outer edges of camp. With the rising moon came the distant howl of coyotes causing the rabbits to bolt about as if they had been struck by lightning.

By early morning, every jackrabbit had disappeared into the dry brush and tules. All was quiet and as I walked to the edge of the camp, I saw a sea of silvery salt grass. The grass waving back and forth reminded me of the waters of the lake near our village.

Each morning, before the heat of the day, we went to the salt grass fields. We broke the dry grass off close to the ground being careful not to shake off the drops of salty liquid that clung to each blade of grass. We put the grass into our baskets leaning it against the side of the basket so the salt drops on the grass would dry. As the sun rose higher in the sky, I could feel the heat beating down on us. Sweat ran down my face and back until my long black hair stuck to my skin. When I looked at my aunt she was looking at me. We both laughed out loud. There were bands of muddy sweat streaked across her face and I knew my face must look the same. I raised my hands to show her where the sharp blades of salt grass had cut my fingers. She raised her hands showing me her many cuts. Without words we agreed that gathering salt grass was hard work.

Later in the day under shade shelters covered with tule mats, we piled small bundles of salt grass on top of elk skins that were spread on the ground. Three or four people sat under each shelter. Using small willow branches each of us lightly tapped a pile of grass. The dry salt would fall from the grass onto the skins. We did this over and over again until we had filled many baskets with salt. After several days it was time to leave the salt grass fields. Each one of us carried a large basketful of salt back to our village.

When we returned home, the women crowded around us waiting to receive a share of salt. Some of the women mixed the salt with water and cooked it into a thick mush. The salt mush was formed by hand into small lumps and kept in clay bowls in each kawe. My aunt gave me a tiny lump of salt and I put it into my mouth. The salty taste made me think of the salt fields and how hard we had worked to bring the salt back to our village.

Chapter Fourteen

Watihte, the Ground Owl

One morning before dawn I was startled by my mother's call. She could not move from her tule mat. During the days that followed, I was filled with worry. I did the chores for both of us and brought food and water to my mother. Each day she slept more and more. Her breathing became heavy and she grew weaker and weaker. Every evening I sat next to my mother and held her hand just as she had held my hand when I was so sick at Mission Santa Inés.

One evening as mother lay on her tule mat with her eyes closed, I rubbed her hands gently. She opened her eyes, looked at me and smiled. After awhile her breathing became very quiet and I knew by the stillness of her body that my mother's spirit was taking the journey to Tihpiknits' Pahn, the Land of the Hereafter.

Sadness clouded my days. In mourning for my mother, I clamped my long black hair between the parts of a split stick and singed off my hair with

a piece of burning bark. I wrapped the hair I had singed off around a large rock. I threw the rock into a deep hole in the river so the hair couldn't be blown by the wind into the hands of the bad spirits. Now, the bad spirits could do me no harm.

As I sat at the edge of the river thinking about my mother, the sound of the breeze swishing through the willow branches filled my mind with memories. I remembered that once a year my tribe and many other neighboring tribes had traveled up the river channel to an ancient campground where a great mourning ceremony was held. I remembered that during the first two or three days while we waited for the other people to arrive, we gathered willow branches and made willow brooms to swish away the loose dirt and smooth a large area of the campground. The swept space would be used for a dance floor. To one side of the dance floor there was a circular pit where the sacred fire would burn until the ceremony ended. During these first few days of preparation, speeches and stories were told every night. One of my favorite stories was about two brothers who shook the tules and made thunder. I liked to hear the storyteller tell the legend of Pú-Muk, the brother who was mean and smashed things and made big thunder. The other brother, Pó-Ton made little thunder. The storyteller would use a loud voice when he spoke of Pú-Muk. When he talked about Pó-Ton he used a small soft voice.

*   *   *

The Legend of the Thunder Twins

In times long ago, there was a baby who was orphaned with no one to take care of him. A she-dog found the baby and took him to her home. She took care of the baby and named him Thunder. He grew rapidly. Soon the child learned to use a bow and arrow.

One day Thunder told his mother that he was lonely and wanted a companion. He told his mother to get a piece of black charcoal and mark him down the middle from head to toe and then throw him into the river. Thunder's mother was upset, but the boy insisted. So his mother did what Thunder asked. She marked the boy and threw him into the river.

At the end of two days, she heard shouting at dawn and saw two boys coming up out of the water. They called to their mother to build a fire for they were cold. She did so and soon the boys were warm and dry. The boys' mother

named the bigger boy Big Thunder and
called him Pú-Muk. She named the
smaller boy Little Thunder and called
him Pó-Ton.

The Thunder Twins stayed with their
mother for some time and went hunting
for her everyday. At last they told their
mother that they were tired of staying on
earth and wanted to go to the sky. She
agreed with the boys. The boys told her
not to be frightened when she heard them
playing in the sky. They told their mother
that they would be very rough and noisy
at times and they might even get mad at
each other. They told her if their noise
frightened her that she should howl.
When she howled, the Thunder Twins
would hear her and realize that they had
scared her. They would stop their noise.

From that time on, when thunder roars
in the sky everyone knows that the
Thunder Twins are playing. The loudest
thunder is made by Pú-Muk. BOOM!
BOOM! BOOM! The softer thunder is
made by Pó-Ton. Ta-ta-ta-boom! When
the noise gets too loud, the mother of the
Thunder Twins howls and the boys stop
their noise.

*   *   *

When all the mourners had arrived at the campground, the mourning ceremony began. Nobody talked. Everything was quiet. When we could just see the evening star, the chief stood in front of the fire and in a loud voice announced that the mourning ceremony would begin. For the next six days, the people danced, sang, and cried to mourn the dead. Each evening the sacred fire blazed as the dancing continued throughout the night. The dancers held offerings of baskets, bows and arrows, and shell necklaces high above their heads as they danced. While the mourners danced, hundreds and hundreds of small beads were thrown in the air by the women. I watched the dancers' quick moving feet as little by little they pounded the beads into the smooth ground. Soon the rhythm of the music called me into the circle of dancers and for a time I danced and became part of the ceremony. In the dark of the evening I remember how the figures of the dancers were black shadows against the orange flames of the fire. On the sixth night the offerings were burned in the sacred fire and the dancing and singing stopped. Everyone waited and listened for the call of Watihte, the ground owl. Before long the wailing screech of Watihte came floating over the night breezes. The screech told us Watihte was calling to the Great Spirit, Tihpiknits, and asking that the spirits of the dead be admitted to Tihpiknits' Pahn. As everyone listened to the sad sound of the owl, the people knew the mourning ceremony was ending. The chief then told all the people who mourned that they could let their hair grow and eat meat once again.

The next morning, their sadness gone, the mourners ran toward the rising sun. Laughing and splashing in the river, they were now free to wash the pitch and charcoal from their faces. A great feast of acorn bread, antelope, elk, jackrabbit, and squirrel ended the mourning ceremony. All the people returned to their own villages until the village chiefs set the time for another mourning ceremony.

I knew that this year when all the tribes traveled to the ancient campground, my uncle would not allow me to go with them and dance at the mourning ceremony. Perhaps next year my uncle would change his mind and I would be allowed to go to the mourning ceremony and dance for my mother.

Chapter Fifteen

The Secret

Now I did my work alone. I worked every day and I did not attend ceremonies or feasts. When it came time for the initiation ceremonies for the girls of the tribe, I was especially sad because these were very important ceremonies that marked the passage of girls from childhood to adulthood. I was now seventeen summers old and had never been part of the girls' initiation ceremonies.

Every year the boys' initiation ceremonies and the girls' initiation ceremonies were a time for feasting, singing, dancing, and games. Friends and relatives attended the ceremonies and gave special gifts. The boys and girls were told the secrets of the tribe. When the ceremonies ended, the young people were no longer considered children. They were ready to take their places as young adults in the tribe. Would I ever know the secrets of my people? Would I ever be part of the girls' ceremonies?

One day as I crouched in the brush watching the

feasting that followed the secret initiation ceremonies for the girls, a woman saw me and I ran away. I ran down the path through the tules to the river. I walked along the banks of the river and suddenly I remembered the old cave that my parents had used as a hiding place when strangers came over the mountain passes to our village. I remembered hiding there many times. Looking for the cave, I pushed patches of dry brush away from the large rocks along the river and when I was almost ready to give up, I heard rustling in some nearby shrubs. Slowly parting the shrubs, I saw the opening to the cave! As I entered the cave I smelled the wet, musty smell I remembered as a child. I sneezed and suddenly above me there was a flutter of wings. Peering into the dim light I saw a large white owl sitting on a rocky ledge above my head. His huge yellow eyes were staring at me. I stood still and soon the owl closed one eye. He didn't seem to mind sharing his cave with me. My eyes grew more accustomed to the dim light in the cave and as I looked around I saw the pictographs that had been painted on the wall of the cave many years ago. I sat down and looked at the drawings. My heart filled with joy and as I had done many years ago my fingers traced the familiar lines of turtles, tule elk, and birds. The pictographs seemed to come to life and I found myself humming the songs my parents had taught me.

Soon I wasn't lonely any more and I knew that the spirits of my parents had brought me to this cave. This, my own place, my place of belonging, was their gift to me. No longer was I filled with sadness for I had left childhood and had become an adult. The cave with the friendly old owl, the sacred songs, and the beautiful pictographs were my own ceremony and would be my very own special secret!

Chapter Sixteen

Pasquala, the One Who Helps Others

A hot breeze stirred the ashes in the firepit as I worked with my aunt preparing the evening meal. Looking up from the fire, I saw a runner from another Yokuts tribe race through the village to our chief's kawe. Soon the chief sent a message to all the men of our village to gather together. I wondered what the men of the tribe were saying to one another. I knew that the runner who had come to our village must have brought important news.

Late that night, my uncle returned to our kawe and I heard him talking to my aunt in a low voice. He said that there was trouble at Mission Santa Inés. One of the Indians at the mission had been badly beaten by the soldados. The word of this beating had spread to two other missions. The neophytes at the Missions Santa Inés, La Purísima, and Santa Barbara said they would no longer take the cruel treatment from the soldados. The neophytes at the missions were asking for help from the Yokuts people. They wanted our people to help them fight the soldados. My uncle said that our chief was organizing a war party from our village to join the war parties from other Yokuts villages. My uncle would lead the warriors from our village on the long journey over the mountains to the mission.

I lay on my tule mat wide awake thinking about the mission and the people who lived there. If there was to be an attack on the mission, I knew it would be soon and sudden and probably at night. I knew the soldados were cruel, but there were many kind and gentle people at the mission. I thought of the padres who had saved my life when I was very young. Should I help them and perhaps save their lives? I stayed awake thinking about my uncle's words and in my mind I struggled with the decision I alone would have to make. I had worked hard to be accepted by my own tribe and I asked myself over and over again what would be the right thing to do. If I went to the mission, it would anger my people. If I didn't go to the mission someone might be hurt because I hadn't warned them. It was a difficult decision, but soon I knew that I must run the long journey through the valleys and over the mountains to warn the padres at the mission.

After what seemed a long time, my uncle left the

kawe and went to the sweathouse with the other men to take sweat baths. The night-long sweat baths would prepare the men's bodies and minds for the attack on the mission. I lay very still on my tule mat waiting until my aunt and everyone in the kawe was sound asleep. The time had come to leave. I quietly got up and filled a pouch with acorn meal, seeds, and dried meat. I slipped like a shadow out of the kawe into the cool night. Closing around me, the darkness became my friend and hid me from the sharp eyes of the camp guard. I could hear the low voices of the men in the sweathouse as I moved quickly toward the tules.

Slowly, but steadily I ran on the path that would lead over the mountain passes to the mission. I remembered this path from the happy days many years ago when I had traveled to the seashore with my parents and my people. Although my tribe had gone to the seashore many times since I had come home, I had never again traveled with them to the ocean. Would I remember the trail? Would I lose my way? Would warriors from my tribe overtake me? I ran faster being careful to watch the trail in front of me and behind me. When I was too tired to go further, I found a place off the trail to sleep. After an hour's rest, I began to run again.

I wound my way upward over the first range of

hills. Late that night I stopped to rest by the river and fell asleep under the spreading branches of an oak tree. When I awoke, I ate a small bit of dried meat from my pouch and the first light of dawn found me beginning the steep climb into the high mountains and pine forests.

The trail was well marked and easy to follow, but soon another trail branched off to the right. Which trail should I take? I peered into the shadowy dark green pines. I saw a large shape on the trail ahead of me. I stopped and stared at it. Coming closer, I saw that it was the old pine tree that had fallen across our path when the earth shook many years before. Now I knew that this was the right trail to take.

I hurried on. My feet were bruised and aching. I stopped only a few times to drink from a brook and to eat the few seeds I had left. If only I could take time to rest!

That night I lay on the ground so tired that I couldn't sleep. Dark clouds hid the moon and cast shadows about me. When I was able, I ran again. For the next two days and nights, sometimes running and sometimes walking, I made my way along the rough and narrow trail.

By now everyone in my village would know that I had left to warn the people at Mission Santa Inés.

The war party might be close behind me and if they found me, they would surely stop me. I had to keep going even though my heart felt like it would burst!

Soon after dawn the trail led downward and I knew that Mission Santa Inés was not too far away. For most of the day I ran as hard as I could and at last I came upon the mission that I had not seen in many years.

The few neophytes that I met in the fields did not recognize me. With failing steps, I made my way to the mission padre. How happy I was to see him. His familiar face made my eyes fill with tears. He greeted me with cries of joy. Unable to speak I couldn't answer his many questions. When I caught my breath, I told the padre that the mission was going to be attacked. The padre took me into the cool corridor and asked a woman to help me into a room. I heard him tell a runner to hurry to a nearby mission and ask for help against the coming attack. The padre gave orders to barricade the mission gates. As the people at the mission prepared for the attack, I could hear the slamming of shutters, locking of doors, and the sound of running feet. I lay on a cot and fell into a fitful sleep.

When I awoke, the padre was sitting by my side. Was it hours later? Days later? I felt very weak, but I understood the padre when he told me that my warning had come in time to save the mission. The padre said that many warriors had come to the mission to burn it down, but because of my warning the people at the mission were prepared to fight. When the warriors realized that their attack was not a surprise they had left.

I lay exhausted on the cot listening to the soft rustle of the padre's robe as he moved across the room. It was hard for me to breathe and my chest was filled with pain. I knew the journey that I had run from the Valley of the Tules to the mission had been too much for me. As the padre held a cup of water to my lips, I could see the kindness in his eyes. I wanted to tell him about my people and my life in the Valley of the Tules.

Slowly, I began to speak. The padre nodded his head when I spoke about my village that lay near the shores of our great blue lake. How beautiful it was when the sun broke through the thick tule fog and bathed the village and lake in warm sunlight. I told about the vast green and brown patches of tules that covered the valley floor like a blanket—tules for Yokuts' homes, tules for Yokuts' clothing, and tules for Yokuts' food—tules that sheltered flocks of birds, ducks, and great herds of elk—tules! tules! tules!

Smiling, the padre listened as I talked about red-winged blackbirds snapping up clouds of buzzing mosquitos, blue herons standing on their stick-like legs in the marshes, and the never ending croak of the bullfrogs. I told him how my father had taught me to find the speckled duck eggs hidden deep in the thick patches of tules and where to find the little fish of the sloughs.

The padre bowed his head when I told him how the elders of the tribe had passed on tribal stories that had been told to the elders when they were young—stories of how and why our people came to be—stories of how we lived in harmony with nature and took only what we needed from the land. I told the padre how my mother and my father had shared their love for the land and animals with me and how they had taught me to respect all that the Great Spirit had given to us.

When I was too weak to continue, the padre told me to rest. I closed my eyes and I heard him say that he understood my love for my people, the Yokuts. He told me he knew how difficult it had been for me to leave my home in the Valley of the Tules to warn the people at the mission. Taking my hands in his, the padre said that the story of my life would be told to many people. He knelt beside my bed. After a long while, he whispered my name. He told me he had named me correctly for I,

Pasquala, was truly the one who loved and helped others.

*   *   *

That evening when the sun sank beyond the hills and the sky turned a crimson red, the call of Wátihte, the ground owl, was heard. His long low wail filled the night air and echoed over the mission. Pasquala's spirit had passed into Tihpiknits' Pahn.

Pronunciation Guide

atolé (ah-toh-LAY)

carreta (kar-RET-tah)
chawit (CHA-wit)
chia (CHEE-ah)
chiton (KY-ton)
Chumash (CHEW-mash)
cuera (koo-WHERE-ah)

hala (HALL-lah)
Hih-sa-Na-us
  (HE-saw-NAW-us)

kawe (COW-wee)
Ki-yu (KEY-you)

ladrillo (lah-DREE-yoh)
Lonewis (LONE-ah-whis)

neophyte (KNEE-oh-fight)

padre (PA-dray)
Pasquala (Pass-KWAL-lah)
Po-Ton (POH-Ton)
presidio (pre-SEE-dee-oh)
Pú-Muk (PU-Muck)

ramada (ra-MAH-dah)

Santa Inés
  (SAHN-tah Ee-NEZ)
Shoshone
  (Show-SHOW-knee)
soldado (sohl-DAH-doh)

Tihpiknits (Tih-PICK-nits)
Toi-uk (TOY-youk)
Tulamnui
  (Too-LAHM-nee-oo)

Watihte (WA-tee-tay)
winatun (WIN-a-ton)

Yokuts (YO-cuts)

Source of Legends

Page 14, *"The Legend of the Ants and the Rattlesnake"* paraphrased from:

Latta, Frank F. *Handbook of Yokuts Indians* (second edition). Santa Cruz, California: Bear State Books, 1977. Page 578.

Page 39, *"The Legend of Tihpiknits and Ki-yu"* paraphrased from:

Latta, Frank F. *Handbook of Yokuts Indians* (second edition). Santa Cruz, California: Bear State Books, 1977. Pages 683-684.

Page 74, *"The Legend of the Thunder Twins"* paraphrased from:

Gayton, A. H. and Newman, Stanley S. *Yokuts and Western Mono Myths.* Volume 5, Number 1. Anthropological Records. Berkeley, California: University of California Press, 1939. Pages 48-50.

Production services and printing by
Blaco Printers, Inc., San Leandro, CA 94577

Bibliography

Chruszch, Karen. *The Yokuts of Kern County.* Bakersfield, California: Kern County Museum, 1987.

Cummins, Marjorie. *The Tache-Yokuts Indians of the San Joaquin Valley.* Fresno, California: Pioneer Publishing Company, 1978.

Da Silva, Owen. *Mission Music of California.* Los Angeles, California: Warren F. Lewis Publishers, 1941.

Faber, Gail and Lasagna, Michele. *Whispers Along the Mission Trail.* Alamo, California: Magpie Publications, 1986.

Faber, Gail and Lasagna, Michele. *Whispers From The First Californians.* Alamo, California: Magpie Publications, 1981.

Garces, Francisco. (John Galvin, Editor). *A Record of Travels in Arizona and California.* San Francisco, California: John Howell Books, 1947.

Gayton, A. H. *Yokuts and Western Mono Ethnography.* Volume 10. Anthropological Records. Berkeley, California: University of California Press, 1948.

Gayton, A. H. and Newman, Stanley S. *Yokuts and Western Mono Myths.* Volume 5, Number 1. Anthropological Records. Berkeley, California: University of California Press, 1939.

Heizer, Robert. *Handbook of the North American Indians: California.* Volume 8. Washington, D.C.: Smithsonian Institution, 1978.

Heizer, Robert. *The Natural World of the California Indians.* Berkeley, California: University of California Press, 1980.

Heizer, R. F. and Whipple, M. A. *The California Indians, A Source Book.* Berkeley, California: University of California Press, 1951.

Kroeber, A. L. *Handbook of the Indians of California.* Berkeley, California: University of California Press, 1923.

Latta, Frank F. *California Indian Folklore.* Shafter, California: F. F. Latta (Bear State Books), 1936.

Latta, Frank F. *Handbook of Yokuts Indians* (second edition). Santa Cruz, California: Bear State Books, 1977.

Powers, Stephen. *Tribes of California.* Berkeley, California: University of California Press, 1900.